◆ In Celebration of ◆

A special book
for your
special day!

Ort & Datum

Name

Wishes

Picture of the day

Name

Wishes

Picture of the day

Name

Wishes

Picture of the day

Name

Wishes

Picture of the day

Name

Wishes

Picture of the day

Name

Wishes

Picture of the day

Name

Wishes

Picture of the day

Name

Wishes

Picture of the day

Name

Wishes

Picture of the day

Name

Wishes

Picture of the day

Name

Wishes

Picture of the day

Name

Wishes

Picture of the day

Name

Wishes

Picture of the day

Name

Wishes

Picture of the day

Name

Wishes

Picture of the day

Name

Wishes

Picture of the day

Name

Wishes

Picture of the day

Name

Wishes

Picture of the day

Name

Wishes

Picture of the day

Name

Wishes

Picture of the day

_____

Name

Wishes

_____

_____

_____

_____

_____

_____

_____

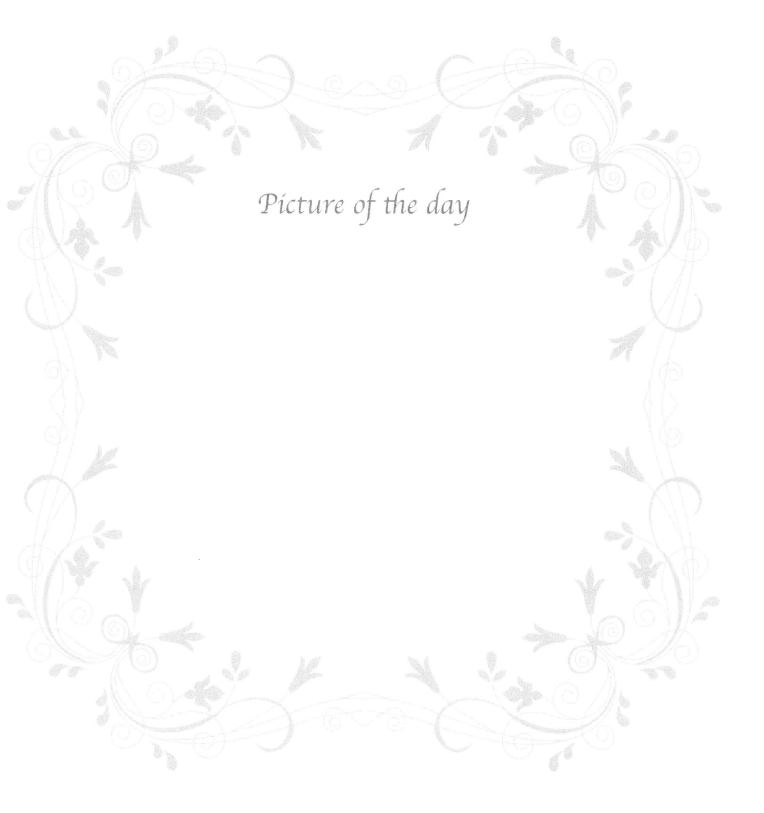

Picture of the day

Name

Wishes

Picture of the day

Name

Wishes

Picture of the day

Name

Wishes

Picture of the day

Name

Wishes

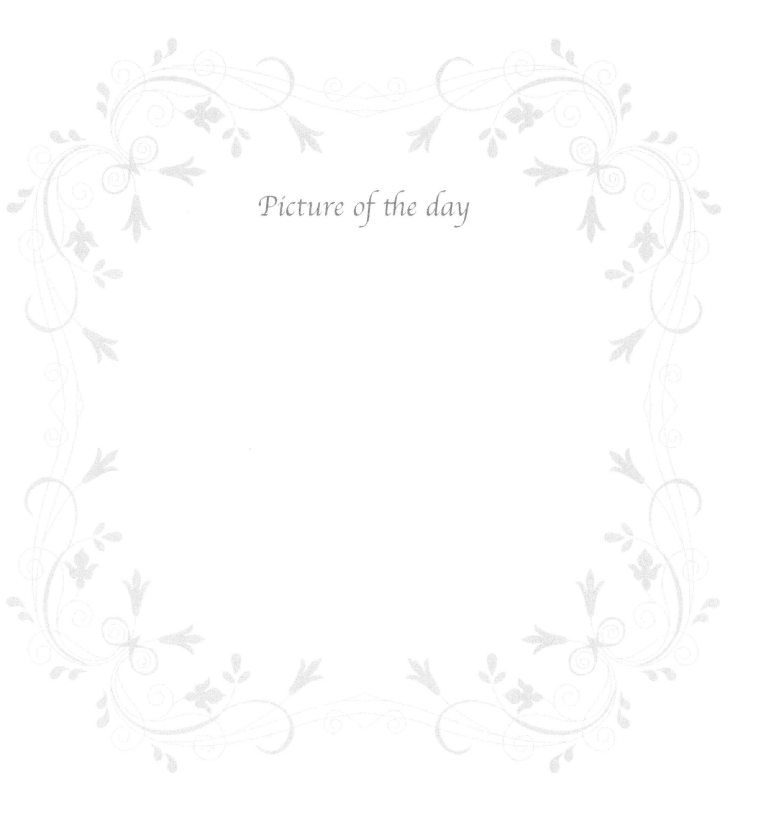

Picture of the day

Name

Wishes

Picture of the day

Name

Wishes

Picture of the day

Name

Wishes

Picture of the day

Name

Wishes

Picture of the day

Name

Wishes

Picture of the day

Name

Wishes

Picture of the day

Name

Wishes

Picture of the day

Name

Wishes

Picture of the day

Name

Wishes

Picture of the day

Name

Wishes

Picture of the day

Name

Wishes

Picture of the day

Name

Wishes

Picture of the day

Name

Wishes

Picture of the day

Name

Wishes

Picture of the day

Name

Wishes

Picture of the day

Name

Wishes

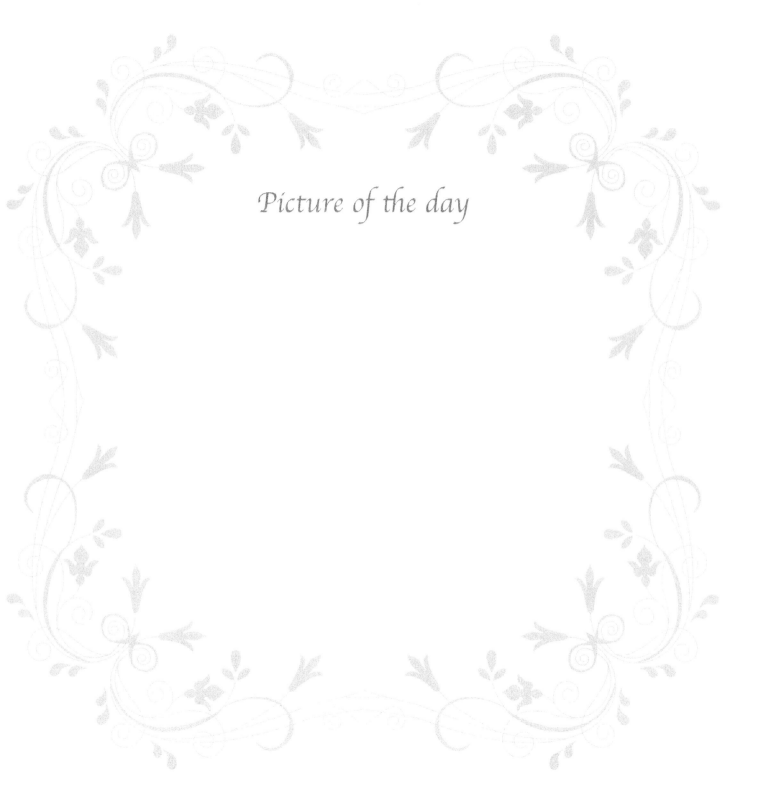

Picture of the day

Name

Wishes

Picture of the day

Name

Wishes

Picture of the day

Name

Wishes

Picture of the day

Name

Wishes

Picture of the day

Name

Wishes

Picture of the day

Name

Wishes

Picture of the day

Name

Wishes

Picture of the day

Name

Wishes

Picture of the day

Name

Wishes

Picture of the day

Name

Wishes

Picture of the day

_____

Name

Wishes

_____

_____

_____

_____

_____

_____

_____

Picture of the day

Name

Wishes

Picture of the day

Name

Wishes

Picture of the day

Name

Wishes

Picture of the day

Name

Wishes

Picture of the day

Name

Wishes

Picture of the day

Name

Wishes

Picture of the day

Name

Wishes

Picture of the day

Name

Wishes

Picture of the day

Name

Wishes

Picture of the day

Name

Wishes

Picture of the day

Name

Wishes

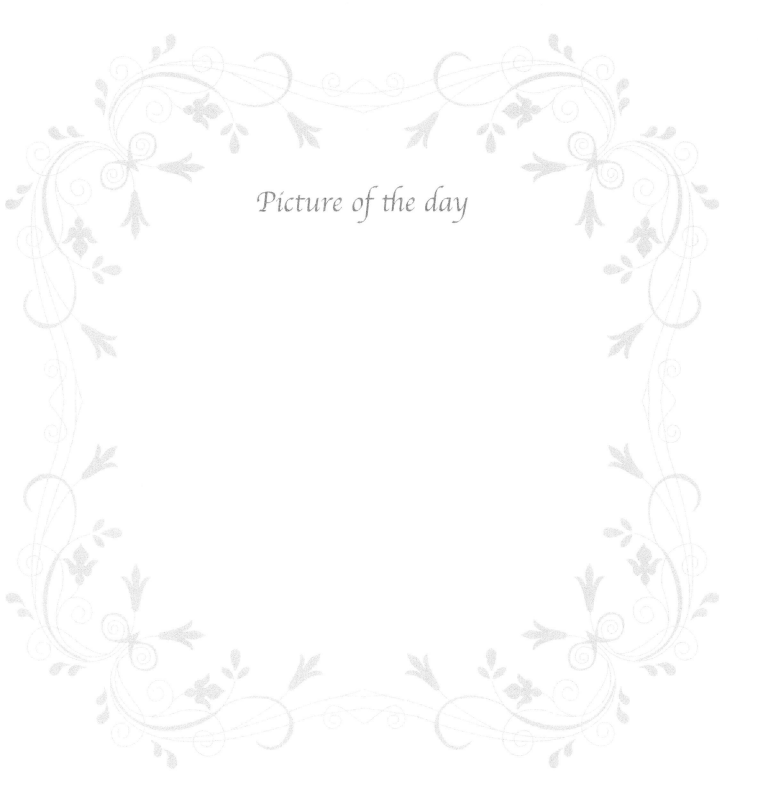

Picture of the day

Name

Wishes

Picture of the day

Name

Wishes

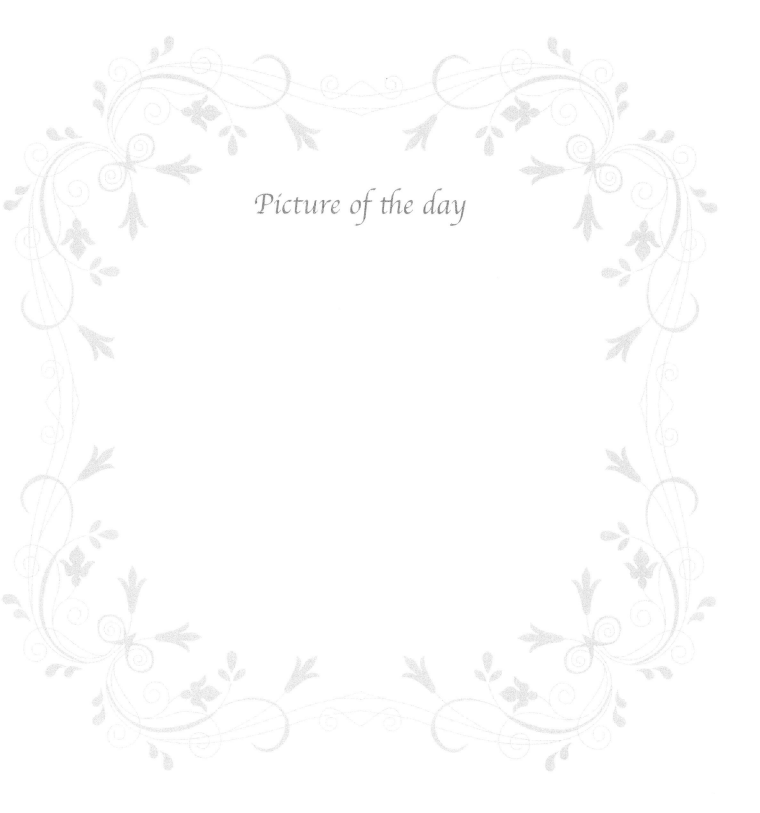

Picture of the day

Name

Wishes

Picture of the day

Name

Wishes

Picture of the day

Name

Wishes

Picture of the day

Name

Wishes

Picture of the day

Name

Wishes

Picture of the day

Name

Wishes

Picture of the day

Name

Wishes

Picture of the day

Name

Wishes

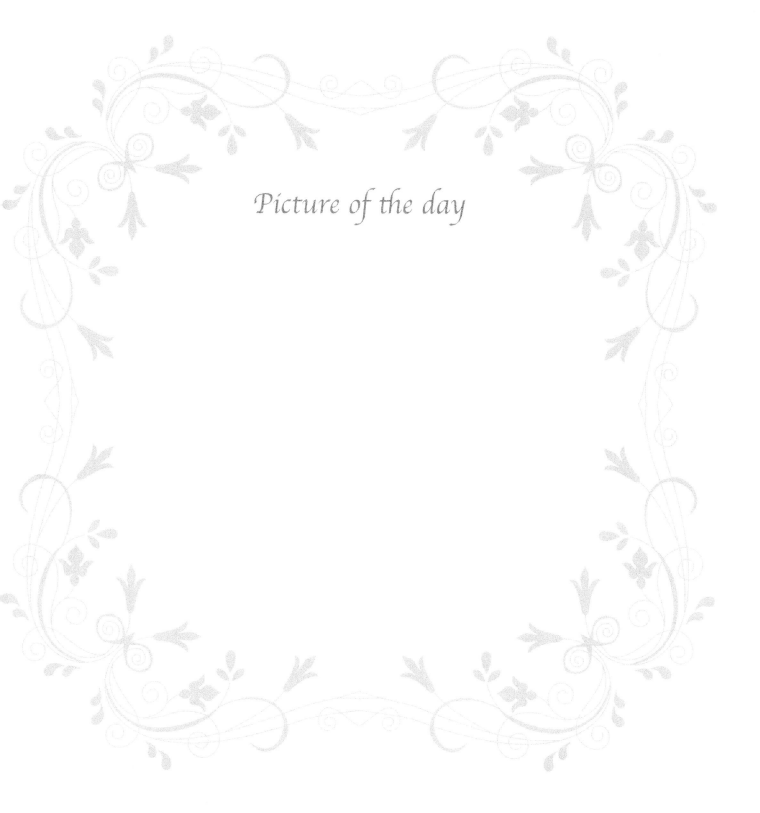

Picture of the day

Name

Wishes

Picture of the day

Name

Wishes

Picture of the day

Name

Wishes

Picture of the day

Name

Wishes

Picture of the day

Name

Wishes

Picture of the day

Name

Wishes

Picture of the day

Name

Wishes

Picture of the day

Name

Wishes

Picture of the day

Name

Wishes

Picture of the day

Name

Wishes

Picture of the day

Name

Wishes

Picture of the day

Name

Wishes

Picture of the day

Name

Wishes

Picture of the day

_____

Name

Wishes

_____

_____

_____

_____

_____

_____

_____

Picture of the day

Name

Wishes

Picture of the day

Name

Wishes

Picture of the day

Made in the USA
Monee, IL
14 April 2023

31874628R00103